Blessing Dave
I just wanted to share with
you my newly published
book. May you be blessed.

Together in Him in
the harvest

Charlie

Heb 10:23

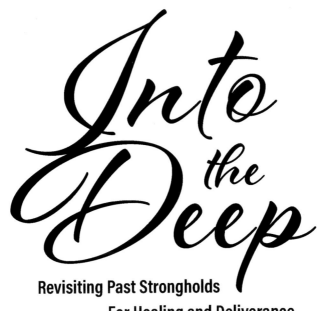

Into the Deep

Revisiting Past Strongholds
For Healing and Deliverance

CHARLIE MOODY

CONTENTS

Endorsements   *vi*

Dedication   *ix*

Acknowledgements   *x*

Foreword   *xi*

Prologue   *xiii*

One THE DEEP PLACES   *1*

Two REVISITING DEEP PLACES   *7*

Three REVISITING DEEP DETOURS   *18*

Four REVISITING DEEPLY LOST OPPORTUNITIES   *27*

Five REVISITING DEEP HOPELESSNESS   *36*

Six REVISITING WHAT DEEPLY MATTERS MOST   *46*

Seven REVISITING DEEPLY LOST LIFE UPGRADES   *55*

Eight RE-VISITATIONS   *65*

Nine DEEP INTIMACY   *70*

Ten DEEPLY BELOVED   *78*

Eleven SEEKING DEEPLY   *86*

Epilogue   *98*

Endorsements

When I began to read Charlie Moody's book, *Into the Deep*, I knew I was in for a special blessing. The blessing was not just the excellent content and personal reflection Charlie brought to the manuscript; it was the blessing of knowing the author. I had the joy of being with Charlie and his wife, Judith Ellen, at their church in Libby, Montana. I got to see Charlie behind the pulpit, with his people, and in the community. He is the real deal in each context. The life stories Charlie shared to illustrate his thoughts tugged on my emotions, both with laughter and tears. Sit down and enjoy this book. I know God will speak to you just as he spoke to me as I moved through each page being saturated in God's love.

-Garris Elkins, author, speaker, and mentor

Into The Deep is a powerful book. I felt God spoke directly to me when I read it, and I believe you will feel the same thing. We all have deep places in our lives – deep old hurts, disappointments, or sadness. This is a book about God's desire to heal those deep places. I encourage you to let him. Read this book.

-Bowen Greenwood, Clerk of the Montana Supreme Court, bestselling author of Christian young adult series, *Sons of Thunder,* and other bestsellers.

"Into The Deep" gives us a "fly on the wall" perspective into the life and times of Charlie Moody. With great candidness, Charlie shares his life with us as Holy Spirit bids him to get out "into the deep". To an equally candid reader, "Into the Deep" will do the same. If you want to stay in shallow water, "Into The Deep", is not for you. If you want to mature and experience an adventuristic life in Christ, this is a good read.

-Michael A. McGovern, Ret. Pastor, Christian Assembly Foursquare Church, Missoula, MT and Ret. District Supervisor, Great Northern District of Foursquare Churches

I have known Charlie and Judith Ellen for over a decade and have seen what a life dedicated to Jesus looks like through them. In his new book, Charlie will take you on a journey that allows you to see what responding to the call of God can produce in a man's life and the transformative power that Holy Spirit has on a community. Charlies' hunger for the presence of God has defined his life and his story will inspire you to go deeper with Jesus.

-Dr. Nick Gough, MTS, D.Min, Foursquare Divisional Leader

Dedication

This book is dedicated to everyone who has struggled to get beyond some deep, negative experience in their past which has, in some measure, become a hinderance to fully realizing their dreams in the present. It is to such "comrades in arms," who continue to press on against such obstacles without surrendering to those deep feelings within, that I proclaim, "There is hope. Do not give up. There is breakthrough; do not wither. Breakthrough has a name, Jesus Christ, and He wants to revisit those deep areas with you for healing. The risk is worth the results. He will not fail. Get ready to launch into the deep stymying areas of your past and know a fresh springboard to your full future and well-being."

Acknowledgements

This book only became a dream realized because of all the Lord has done with me and in me. It is under His inspiration these words were penned. And it was the unwavering belief and support for me from my loving partner of 40-plus years, Judith Ellen, who never ceased encouraging me to write. I love you more than you will ever know. Finally, I want to thank the countless brothers and sisters in the body of Christ who have helped mold and shape my life. You guys rock and… are a rock. Love ya.

Foreword

I was one of Charlie Moody's "sheep" for several years while he served as shepherd at Abundant Life Ministries in Havre, Montana. His presence in my life during that time set off the greatest, longest, most life-changing period of spiritual growth I had ever had and that continues to this day. I don't know if Charlie is actually an apostle, but I know he is connected to heaven and has a vision for earth that he constantly imparts. I don't know that Charlie is actually a prophet, but I know Charlie brings words of life and encouragement to individuals that are straight from the heart of God. Charlie is a teacher, illuminating the scriptures to his hearers. Charlie is a pastor, his love for people and compassion for their hurts is extraordinary. In the pages of this book, you will find evidence of all of these, and you will find it packaged in the words of humility, grace, and gratefulness that encompasses everything Charlie says and does. As the title indicates, Charlie's personal life experiences with God are deep. They anchor him to his Rock. They remind him always of the great love, compassion, sacrifice, and commissioning that Jesus offered Charlie on his living room floor so many years ago, and that Charlie has never lost sight of. I knew some of the stories in this book before I read it. Some of the stories were new, and they touched me, deeply. They reminded me to remember my testimonies also. God wastes nothing. He gets you ready. He loves to unfold your path and His goodness before you. Charlie's stories are a marvelous illustration of those principles. I hope you enjoy this book.

Kris Hansen, former State Senator,
Montana State Legislation
Avid Moody Supporter
Future Political Influencer and Governmental
Culture Changer
Or possibly, if Charlie has his way,
Madam President

Prologue

98-year-old Ray Lambert was an Army medic in 1944 and was part of the D-Day invasion of Normandy. Though repeatedly injured during the assault, he courageously saved many of his fellow comrades-in-arms, before being extricated from the battle to be hospitalized. Upon returning home, having witnessed so much combat carnage, he spent most of the rest of his life burying the memories inside, never talking about the suffering he witnessed.

70 years later, Ray became a part of a group of soldiers and world leaders who began to make a yearly pilgrimage to revisit Omaha Beach, the site of the D-Day landing. A town above the landing site had dedicated a plaque, embedded in a concrete slab, which simply said, "Ray's Rock". It was to commemorate the site of

where, decades earlier, Ray had sheltered many of his wounded fellow soldiers during the assault. Revisiting the site became a place of closure and healing for old memories. He said of his revisits, "The way I'd like to be remembered was a guy who was willing to die for my family and country, and a good soldier and a good person.

We all have histories, events and incidents, which have left lasting impressions on us for either good or bad memories. The good memories when revisited tend to carry within them a warmth and nostalgia that one can freely bask in the remembrances of. The less than fond memories, depending on the depth of the hurt or disappointment, are often not so readily revisited. Everyone tends to embrace "warm and fuzzy" while seeking to avoid pain and disappointment. Yet, all too often, it is those deeper, darker places of our memories that most need healing and repair. It is in recognition of the necessity for inner healing through revisiting that this book is written. Much of it evolved from my own personal areas of deeply experienced past events and the inner "strongholds" that emerged against my moving forward in other areas of life.

Stagnation is never a part of the Lord's plans for our lives; He always intends to move us forward and upward to greater opportunities and experiences.

"For I know the plans I have for you," says the Lord, "They are plans for good and not disaster, to give you a future and a hope." (Isaiah 29:11 NLT)

The deep negative events of our past, left unattended and not dealt with, have a marked tendency to hold us back from the fuller things of God. The purpose in writing this book is to demonstrate the Lord's desire to revisit such areas to render hope for hopelessness, purpose for aimlessness, and healing for hurt. This book is not inclusive of everything that has become a deeply held stronghold of everyone's past, rather, it is a compilation of such experiences from my life which demonstrate the love, goodness, and willingness of the Lord to "set the captive free." It is my hope that you will be emboldened to revisit those deep areas of your life with the Lord for healing and freedom that you will be freshly edified, and He would be glorified.

Charlie Moody

One

THE DEEP PLACES

So it was, as the multitude pressed about Him to hear the word of God, that He stood by the Lake Gennesaret, and saw two boats standing by the lake, but the fishermen had gone from them and were washing their nets. Then He got into one of the boats, which was Simon's, and asked to put out a little from the land. And He sat down and taught the multitudes from the boat.

When He had stopped speaking, He said to Simon, "Launch out into the deep and let down your nets for a catch."

But Simon answered and said to Him, "Master, we have toiled all night and caught nothing; nevertheless at Your word I will let down the net." And when they had done this, they caught a large number of fish, and their net was breaking. So they signaled to their partners in the other boat to come and help them. And they came and filled both the boats, so that they began to sink. When Simon Peter saw it, he fell down at Jesus' knees, saying, "Depart from me, for I am a sinful man, O Lord!"

For he and all who were with him were astonished at the catch of fish which they had taken; and so also were James and John, the sons of Zebedee, who were partners with Simon. And Jesus said to Simon, "Do not be afraid. From now on you will catch men." So when they had brought their boats to land, they forsook all and followed Him.

Luke 5:1-11 (New King James Version)

In 30-plus years of ministry, I've preached this passage of scripture numerous times. It's almost always been along the common threads of "launching into the deeper things of Christ" or "Simon comes to the end of himself." There is truth in these approaches, but a recent revelation brought another understanding to me concerning this passage and its personal application to each and every one of us.

I know Simon Peter was a fisherman; it was his livelihood. We don't know how successful he was at his occupation because I don't read anywhere in the scripture where he ever caught a fish without Jesus' intervention. I'm sure he was better at fishing than scripture portraits, but it's not evident from what we read.

Case in point: Luke 5:1-11. Simon Peter has just finished a long, arduous, fruitless night of fishing. He came back into shore to call it a day, clean his nets, and go home for some much needed sleep. On the shoreline, a short distance away, Jesus is preaching and teaching the word of God. As more and more people are drawn to hear Him, He finds Himself being backed into the shallows of the lake. Immediately He calls upon Simon Peter's services. Simon moves his fishing boat into a position where Jesus climbs aboard and now safely continues His ministry. Simon quietly sits and listens from the bow of the boat.

Finally Jesus finishes, turns to Simon Peter and tells him to "launch into the deep and fish again." Here's where it gets good. I can imagine Simon Peter sitting there exhausted, thinking to himself, *"You've got to be kidding. You can't possibly be serious."* Then the verbal protests begin (paraphrased), "Aw, come on man, we did this thing all night, I don't want to do it again now." Then their eyes connect, and Simon Peter caves in. "All right, all right. It doesn't matter. Nevertheless, whatever You say," and together they launch out into the deep.

It's here, at this point that it all starts to come together for Simon Peter and, consequently, us as well.

This "deep" was more than just a fishing spot. It represented a spiritual area as well, which, for Simon Peter, was a place in his life of deep frustration, deep failure, and possibly even deep anger. This one fishing spot had denied him success for all his time and labor. I'm sure there was some resentment in revisiting such a spot of deep fruitlessness. Of course, this time it wasn't so; such a large harvest of fish came forth from the lake that the boat could not contain the catch.

What the Lord began to show me was this: Simon Peter was about to receive a fresh spiritual commissioning from the Lord, one that would forever alter the course of his life. Before that could happen, the deep failures of the night before, and possibly many other fruitless nights as well, needed healing.

Know this, brothers and sisters, as with Simon Peter, Jesus loves to revisit the "deep places" of our lives, the deep hurts, deep betrayals, deep angers, deep frustrations, deep failures, and deep losses, all with the intended purpose of bringing forth healing and deliverance. All too often our spiritual destinies are halted by our failure to deal with the "deep places" of defeat from our past. If we are to ever realize Kingdom success in the advancements and commissioning of the Lord, we, with the Lord, must deal with any prior unresolved deep hindrances which might block such possibilities.

By bringing forth "the catch of a lifetime" in Simon Peter's "deep place" of fruitlessness, Jesus was healing him of any vestiges of prior failure and giving assurances of future destiny opportunities. He'll do the same for you and me.

When, after all his protesting, Simon Peter says in resignation, "Nevertheless," he unknowingly hits the key to it all. The one who desires to revisit our "deep places" is truly the Lord of "Never the Less" and "Always the More."

Two

REVISITING DEEP PLACES

"...*arise, Go up to Ai. I have given it into your hand...*"

Joshua 8:1 (New Heart English Bible)

After experiencing a resounding victory over the city of Jericho, the children of Israel had a deeply humiliating defeat at the hands of a little town, Ai. This was because of sin in their midst. Once that was revealed and dealt with, they revisited the place of deep defeat and knew a great victory.

My wife and I came to the Lord in 1984, crying out in our living room to know the reality of a living God. Our history up to that point had been one checkered with alcohol and drug abuse coupled with years of involvement in a New Age group for which I had been a touring lecturer. I also had my own weekly newspaper column, which I frequently used to debase Christians.

Prior to our salvation, everything we were previously involved in began to fall apart. We didn't realize it at the time, but God was setting us up for an encounter with Him. We had come to a place of feeling void inside of anything worthwhile. Then through a series of divinely orchestrated events, we found ourselves sitting in our living room one night, desperate for a lifestyle change. Up to that point, we had tried everything but God. In despair, I remember turning to my wife and saying, "If this God is true, maybe He can do something with me." I fell to my knees and cried out, "If You are real, show me. I can't go on like this."

BAM.

I equate what happened next as being hit between the eyes with a spiritual two by four. I would later come to call it my "Damascus Road Experience," based on what the apostle Paul experienced in the Book of Acts

9:1-9. When I came up off the floor, I was totally and marvelously different. It took my wife, Judith Ellen, a little longer to experience that moment. Being raised Jewish meant never accepting Jesus as God. Her transition was more gradual but still very real.

I was so impacted by what had occurred that I was out on the streets the next day evangelizing, not even aware of what I was doing. I knew nothing but what Jesus had done in my life and my entire theology at that point was: "You've got to know this Jesus, it's amazing." I remember people looking at me with puzzled expressions, frequently asking, "What do you mean?" to which I would shrug my shoulders and give the only answer I knew, "Ya just gotta know this Jesus. It's wonderful."

In those early days and weeks of our newfound life, we had no one to instruct us; we questioned what should be our next move. I remember very clearly Judith Ellen suggesting, "Maybe we should go to a church or something. I think that's what others do who believe in Jesus." That sounded wise, so we set about figuring out which church we should attend. We finally decided on a mainline denominational church in town based on the fact that we knew the pastor socially; he was at some of the same parties we used to attend (should have been a tip-off).

So, off we went for the next five Sundays to faithfully attend his church. We were so excited about our newly found life that we didn't know what to expect or look for in a church. Yet even in our naïve innocence, something didn't seem right. During those initial five weeks, only one person in this church welcomed us. We remained invisible to everyone else. We were so giddy with Jesus we barely noticed. One thing that did strike us as odd was the fact that in the five weeks we attended, we never heard the bible read once; they were doing an in depth study of the denomination's history. We also tried to get involved in some church activities but were never taken up on our offer.

It was then that the Holy Spirit stepped into the picture and met us at a level we could understand Him. Every Sunday during that time, we would go home after services, take everything out of the refrigerator, and lay it out on the kitchen counter. We would then proceed to gorge ourselves to the point of discomfort. We had never done anything like this before. Finally, on the fifth week of this behavior, I turned to Judith Ellen, "Can I ask you a question? Why are we doing this?" She stopped her eating, looked at me, and answered, "I don't know. All I know is that I am so hungry."

Again... BAM.

It was as though light bulbs were going off in my head as the Holy Spirit suddenly made us aware that what we were doing by eating so ravenously was but a physical manifestation of a spiritual hunger, a hunger we felt at not being nurtured and fed in our church experience. We were such "newbies" in the faith that we really didn't realize that it was the Holy Spirit bringing us this understanding, but we understood that something had to change.

We decided that maybe we should try another church and see if it was different. I arranged to meet with the pastor over coffee to inform him of our decision, knowing it would be difficult to tell him. I felt extremely awkward... until he gave me his response. He looked at me and said, "It is better that you both leave because you would never be welcome in our church anyway. You, with your New Age background and your wife being Jewish... well, you'd never be accepted."

I left our meeting shocked at the callousness with which he said what he did. I felt deep rejection and hurt. Both my wife and I were stunned at how deeply this negatively affected us. Our first experience with Christianity and church were a bust, and we knew it. For a while, we struggled to find our next move. Judith Ellen finally proposed one day, "Maybe we should pray." Neither one of us really knew what prayer looked like but knew that Christians did it to figure things out. So we offered up the most casual, matter-of-fact, genuine prayer that we could muster. Surprisingly, at least to me, we both felt that we were being led to go to a Pentecostal church in town, where I had heard the people were "crazy." After some hesitancy on my part, we attended the following Sunday. When we walked through the foyer doors into the sanctuary, literally, the entire church came to greet us. We were home.

Fast-forward about 15 years. We were now in pastoral ministry with the Foursquare Gospel Church. Our journey had taken us to an entirely different community than where we had begun our new life in Christ. It was a time of great personal and corporate growth as well. At Thanksgiving of that 15th year, a powerful and miraculous experience occurred in our fellowship. It was the Sunday before Thanksgiving, and I had just returned from two weeks of being in the Brownville Revival in Pensacola, Florida. My life had been radically changed by the experience of encountering the presence of God in such a tangible way. I had never known Him like that before. All the way home from the revival I kept challenging the Lord, "If Your presence will not come with me the way I now know You, then ditch this plane and take me home. I would rather go home to be with You than go back to dry, dead religion." I was emphatic and serious.

Because I made it home, I fully expected that God was with me as I had asked. I felt led to preach that Sunday on the topic; "God is a God who still answers by fire!" My text was from 1 Kings 18, Elijah on Mount Carmel and his challenge to bring the people of Israel back to the Lord. In the account, they are moved to return when the fire of the Lord's presence consumes the altar sacrifice with the altar as well. With this outward display from the Lord, the people in mass return to Him. I preached that day with a fresh conviction on my heart for what I felt the Lord wanted. At the end of the message, I challenged the people, "Unlike Elijah and his animal sacrifice, we are called to present ourselves to the Lord as living sacrifices (Romans 12:1). This I know, if you will but present yourself this day at this altar, He is still the God who answers by fire!"

In that moment of time, the entire direction of a majority of that Sunday's attendees and the church itself were altered forever. As people rose from their seats and began to approach the altar, a heavy, weightiness filled the atmosphere. No one could make it to the altar. Wave upon wave of God's presence washed over the congregants. No one remained untouched. People were falling to the ground everywhere in the sanctuary. Some were weeping, others were laughing as God was falling with fresh fire of His presence upon His people. That same overwhelming presence even hit the children's Sunday school class; five gave their hearts to the Lord immediately. I had to be held up by the elders in our church, my legs would no longer support me. This went on for hours and ended with people begging to come back that evening to be in His presence. This began an additional evening service, which we had never had before. That evening when we came back, there were 35 new people at the service; word had gotten out that something unusual yet special was happening. Thus began a year and a half move of God in our fellowship where many were saved, healed, and delivered. Everything became fresh and new.

It was during this time that the Lord birthed a new ministry in my life titled: Fresh Wind Ministries. It became an outreach ministry to other churches that desired to share in our experience. Besides our regular pastoral duties in our home church, my wife and I found ourselves being called out to other churches to share the "fire." We found ourselves frequently visiting other churches.

One night, we received a call from a young pastor who had been holding community wide worship services in his church on Sunday nights. The worship teams were made up of various musicians from a multitude of the churches in his community. He was very excited and told us, "I felt that there had to be more than what we were doing, so I asked the Lord for direction. The next day, someone was telling me about what God is doing with your church and I felt that this was an answer from the Lord. I want to ask both of you if would you come and preach revival on Sunday night." We looked at each other, smiling in disbelief. This young pastor was the new minister of the church that had so deeply hurt us and rejected us when we were first saved. We said, "Yes!"

That Sunday night, the church was packed, standing room only. We were given "carte blanche" to do whatever we felt God wanted. After the regular time of worship, I preached. I don't even remember what I preached, but at the end of the message, I gave an altar call for salvation and healing. God's glory filled the sanctuary, and once again, no one made it to the altar. Pews and aisles were littered with people prostrated, crying out to the Lord. We found out later, they hadn't had an altar call in this church in over 80 years!

It was extremely late when we left that night, having prayed for as many people as possible. It was impossible to not feel the personal elation of partnering with God who loves us so incredibly. That evening, one of the greatest healings received was the one my wife and I felt sweep over our lives, as God, in great grace, love, and joy, revisited with us a "deep place" of unresolved rejection, restoring us to a strong sense of worthiness and personal value.

I've learned over these last thirty years of ministry that God does not like to leave unfinished ends in our lives. It doesn't matter how long, or where, or how He chooses to do it, but He loves to revisit our "deep places" where hurt, rejection, frustration, unworthiness, and so many other negative experiences have sought to create strongholds of discouragement in our lives. It's never a fearful thing to revisit such areas with Him, though it may not feel that way initially. His purpose, however, is to bring deep healing and deliverance every time. Proverbs 3:5-6 (The Passion Translation) tells us: Trust in the Lord completely, and do not rely on your own opinions. With all your heart rely on Him to guide you, and He will lead you in every decision you make.

It brings great assurance to know that He doesn't just start us on a journey where, if things go wrong, we are supposed to "put on our big boy or big girl pants" and tough it out. He's an ever loving Savior who is both the Author of the journey and the Finisher as well (Hebrews 12:2). What He begins, He will see through to completion.

Three

REVISITING DEEP DETOURS

Then Jephthah fled from his brothers and dwelt in the land of Tob... when the people of Ammon made war against Israel that the elders of Gilead went to get Jephthah from the land of Tob.

Judges 11:3,5 (New King James Version)

Forced by circumstances not of his choosing, Jephthah left his homeland to sojourn in a foreign place. He was not where he should have been, having taken a deep detour from his ultimate destiny. It wasn't until sometime later that he returned to where he should have been.

When we were first going into pastoral ministry in Montana, we encountered an obstacle. Our district superintendent fully recognized the calling on our lives, but informed us that at that time he did not have a place for us in his district. His offered solution was that Judith Ellen and I pray, and he and his board would pray, that the Lord would reveal a possible location for us. We spent a considerable time searching out the heart of the Lord for a place to serve Him in ministry. Several sites crossed our thoughts but didn't quite click. Then one day, while in prayer, the town of Libby, Montana seemed to register as a clear possibility.

Excited, I called our superintendent to inform him of where I thought the Lord wanted us to go. It all seemed perfect as there was yet to be a Foursquare church established there. I was sure in my heart that this was it. He said that he and his board would pray about it and get back to us.

About a week later, he called and said, "I know you believe that this is God's choice place for you to begin your ministry, but let me run something by you for your consideration. I have on my board a man who used to live in Libby. He informed me that Libby is very near a great deal of White Supremacist activity. He felt that this being your first opportunity as pastors, and your wife being as outspoken a Jewish believer as she is, that you might draw some very difficult and unwanted attention. He doesn't think it would be a good idea… and I agree."

I sat there stunned for a moment, realizing that what I truly felt was the Lord's choice for us had just slipped away and disappeared. Whatever road lay ahead for us suddenly was taking a deep detour and going in a different direction. It was back to the spiritual drawing board to find a location for our pastoral call.

At the time of our seeking a place to go, we were also attending and serving the Havre Foursquare Gospel Church, which had started only a year prior. One day, the pastor approached me during this time and said, "My wife and I feel that our call really isn't pastoral in nature but more of pioneering, starting new churches. We're moving to do just that, and we feel that you and Judith Ellen are to be the pastors here."

I had never had aspirations toward Havre and had even prayed, "*Lord, send us anywhere but Havre,*

Montana." But I believe the Lord knew we had something that we needed to work out, so guess what? That's right, Havre became our first location for ministry for the next 23 years.

It was a time of great personal growth; I even came to love Havre and the people. We had witnessed so much of the Lord's miraculous hand covering those years, even, as stated before, we experienced a mighty move of God. I had grown quite comfortable in our little community and imagined us being there for the rest of our life.

Again, fast-forward 23 years. I'm 65 then and not looking for any major changes. One day, we received a communique from our district headquarters to all the churches informing us of a Foursquare church in Kalispell, Montana that had an opening for a senior pastor. The request was that if we had any prospective candidates from our fellowship that would qualify for the position, to see if they would be interested. We didn't, but felt a strange urge to consider this opportunity for ourselves. It went against every "comfort zone instinct" I had for where we currently were ministering. Yet we felt impelled to investigate and pursue the possibility. After much prayer, we threw our proverbial hats into the candidate pool.

Several weeks later, we received a phone call from our district headquarters informing us that they had received our application. They thanked us but informed us that there was no way we would even be considered because the vacated pastoral position was to be filled by someone younger; the church felt a mandate to reach youth. I honestly felt relieved but questioned why the Lord would have so impressed us to pursue an opportunity we would never be able to get. But that wasn't the end of the conversation. They further said, "Even though you don't qualify, we still have to interview you because you put in an application." Their suggestion was that I attend a district conference in several weeks in Missoula, Montana. While there, they would interview me. I agreed even though I didn't see the sense of it.

At the conference, I met a friend over lunch who was the former pastor in Libby, the town we had thought we would launch our pastoral ministry from 23 years earlier. About five years before this conference luncheon, he had invited me to Libby to conduct a weekend evangelism outreach to which I readily went. As we talked, and he told me that Libby had been without a pastor for the last year.

Eventually lunch was over, and I had my interview. I sat in a room with three district administrators who cordially asked a variety of questions. It was all pure formality until I was asked, "How would you categorize your ministry style?" With my lunch time conversation fresh on my mind, I began to tell them that it was like when I ministered in Libby for that weekend outreach. I began to elaborate, when suddenly one of the interviewers interrupted me and asked me why I was talking about Libby, Montana. I explained the conversation that I had just had with the former pastor at lunch and how Libby was fresh on my mind. The rest of the interview concluded as we all knew it would. I would not be their choice, but they thanked me for coming in.

The next day, the conference ended and I was headed to my car when I was stopped by one of the interviewers from the day before.

"Charlie, after you left the interview, we all felt a strong leading to ask you if you and Judith Ellen would prayerfully consider taking the Libby church."

I smiled and agreed that I would pray about it, but inside I was shrugging my shoulders, sluffing off even the notion of considering Libby. 23 years after the fact had jaded me to the idea that Libby had ever been anything but a deep mistake, a deeply faulted perception of where God wanted us to pastor. Strangely, all the way home, I could not shake off thinking about what I had been offered. As hard as I tried, I could not dissuade myself from thinking about Libby.

When I arrived home, I immediately told Judith Ellen what had been proposed. She had the same reaction as me. We both had dismissed the idea of a move to Libby as a deep sense of missing what we thought was God's direction for us 23 years earlier to not hearing God accurately. The fact that we had grown quite comfortable in our present pastorate was also a contributing factor to our reluctance to even garner the thought of moving and beginning all over.

God, however, had other ideas in mind for us, and for the next two weeks we wrestled and prayed but could not dismiss Libby from our thoughts.

It was Monday, our day off, and we decided to have lunch at our favorite Chinese restaurant. We pulled into the mall parking lot, shut off the engine, undid our seatbelts, and looked at each other.

"Ready?" I asked, smiling at her. We both sat back in our seats and just looked at each other. A strange silence passed between us. Neither of us could open the car door to get out. It wasn't that the doors wouldn't open, but rather more like we couldn't go forward in that moment. It was as though time stood still. A strong sense of surrender and resignation washed over us; I knew the "wrestling match" about Libby was over. Sheepishly, I looked at her and asked, "We know, don't we?" She shook her head in affirmation, as tears began to well up in both our eyes. There was nothing to contest; God had won, and we had surrendered. In that moment, we both realized we had won as well. All our comfortable excuses and contrived arguments faded away before a fresh renewed sense of divine purpose and destiny.

Holding hands in the car, we pledged ourselves in that moment to His plans for us. "By life or by death, we will be Your servants in Libby, Montana."

I immediately heard the words in my heart, "*Get ready for the adventure of a lifetime!*" Judith Ellen heard, "*Let the adventure begin!*"

God had brought us full circle. We realized we had heard God accurately; we were meant initially to go to Libby. All the reasons that had originally been offered as to why it wasn't a favorable idea had all later been dispelled as wrong; it was not a White Supremacist town. The deep sense of missing God's direction was revisited with vindication and healing that we had heard Him correctly.

Sometimes it's hard to move forward toward the fulfillment of one's destiny when you're not where you're supposed to be. We end up living a life of "what ifs" or, even worse, moving in directions toward a destination and taking detours that lead us off course. It doesn't mean that where you end up can't have meaning and purpose (After all, Havre was a wonderful place to see God's work lived out), but what if it isn't the exact intended destiny for one's life?

If you have a lost destiny or destination in your life – a place that your spirit still resonates with whenever you think of it – then perhaps that's the Holy Spirit keeping the dream alive. You have only to ask the Lord, the one who says, "Launch into that sense of deep detours, and let's discover together whether it's time to revisit and get back on course. I know the way because I am the way."

Four

REVISITING DEEPLY LOST OPPORTUNITIES

"Simon, son of Jonah, do you love Me more than these?" He said to Him, "Yes, Lord, You know that I love You."

John 21:15 (English Standard Version)

Three times Peter is asked the same question of Jesus. This all occurred after Jesus' resurrection. Before His crucifixion, Jesus had prophesied that Peter would deny Him three times. Peter vehemently refuted the idea that such a thing would ever happen, committing instead to be with Jesus whatever happened. At Jesus' arrest, all the disciples scattered except Peter, who kept his distance to avoid being recognized as a follower. Later that evening when confronted as to his identification as a disciple of Jesus, he denied the fact three times, seeking to distance himself from involvement with the Lord. Immediately, he remembered the prophecy and was filled with remorse; the moment for faithfully standing by his commitment to Jesus was suddenly deeply lost.

In John 21, we witness Jesus revisiting Peter's deep sense of a lost moment, an irretrievable, seemingly forever-gone opportunity. Each of Jesus' three questions concerning Peter's love of Him was a revisiting and restoration of Peter's deeply lost moment.

I've never really asked the Lord of things for myself, but there was this one time. It was about my 20th year in pastoral ministry. A conference was coming to the Seattle area which featured some of the remaining people from the Hebrides Revival in northern Scotland back in the early 1950s. Being a student of that revival, I immediately sought from the Lord a confirmation to attend the conference. I felt that I was to go and began to make plans to be there.

This all came about during a time of unprece-dented growth and excitement in the church. Things seemed as though they couldn't possibly go wrong. I had no idea of the turmoil that was creeping into our midst undiscerned. We had a person in attendance with some unsavory desires to see us ousted and him-self installed as pastor of our church. Slowly, almost imperceptibly, he was making alliances with vari-ous key people in the church. He would find and do favors for them, garnering their support. Gradually, he began creating doubts about my integrity, even going so far as to slander me with conjured lies. The atmosphere in the church began to shift from one of growth, nurturing, and maturity to one of suspicion and uncertainty. At some point in all of this, I became aware of what was transpiring. My first reaction was to confront this nefarious threat head-on. The Lord, however, stopped me, telling me not to defend myself, that He would be my vindicator.

At no time have I ever been so tested in minis-try. I couldn't see how the Lord was going to do what He said. Days turned into weeks without anything changing. It was getting worse. It was nearing the time of the conference, and I no longer felt the lux-ury of being able to attend; I felt I couldn't possibly leave the church at a time like this. So I cancelled my reservation, feeling my opportunity was deeply lost. I remember crying out in anger to the Lord, "What gives? I never ask for anything for myself except this one time, and now I have to give it up?"

I was devastated. The church was sliding into turmoil, and I deeply lost something of great value that could never be restored. I struggled for weeks to maintain trust and faith in what the Lord had said He would do. I was losing the battle.

It was at the very time that the conference was going on in Seattle that I decided to attend the weekly pastors' prayer meeting in town. I went feeling depressed and dejected, not really wanting to be there. At that prayer gathering there was a person in attendance that none of us knew. He was a travelling evangelist, going from Minneapolis to Seattle. The night before, his motorhome had broken down in our town of Havre. He didn't know anybody in our town, so he called a friend back in Minneapolis who referred him to a pastor friend in our community, who was part of our prayer group. He ended up staying overnight with the pastor, who invited him to join our prayer group while his motorhome was being repaired. It wasn't very long before this evangelist began to share

wondrous stories he had witnessed of the Lord's supernatural hand at work all over the world. We all sat in
rapt attention, listening to the incredible accounts of
the miraculous work of God. At some point in his
sharing, it came out that he was a travelling evangelist
who was called by the Lord to the United States from
Scotland. I remember thinking how strange that was
given the nature of my lost opportunity to partake of
the Hebrides Revival of Scotland Conference.

When the hour was over, everyone began to leave.
I, however, felt that I needed to ask this evangelist if he
would pray for me. He was glad to accommodate my
request, and together we moved into the sanctuary of
the church we were meeting in. As he laid hands on
me, he began to pray. Prophecy and words of knowledge began to flow.

"I see you at the steerage wheel of an old, big sail
ship. You're in the midst of a massive, violent storm.
The sails are tattered and torn. You're doing everything you can to keep the ship on course. It's taking all
your strength and…. you feel like you're all alone; that
there is no one with you on board."

At this point, I'm on my knees sobbing uncontrollably. Everything he said was exactly how I felt.
He continued (mind you, he knew nothing of what I

was going through), "The Lord would say to you that you are not alone; there are multitudes with you on board – you just can't see them. Oh, one more thing (he did not know of my lost opportunity): You could not go and receive what Scotland had for you, so God brought Scotland to you."

When he finished praying, I remember feeling a strong sense of relief and assurance. The Lord had used this man to convey the understanding that God knew exactly what I was going through. I left the prayer meeting feeling emotionally undergirded by this knowledge. Unfortunately, I was still left with the unresolved issues evolving in the church.

That evening, we had our regular mid-week service. There were more people than usual because everyone at this point was anxious to understand what was going on. They were all hoping that I would break my silence and begin to address the undercurrent of issues working their way through the church. The man responsible for all this was not there that night. I remember looking out at all the faces staring at me. I wanted desperately to just defend myself and verbally strike out against my detractor. I didn't, however, because of my promise to the Lord. Instead I shared this:

"I know that you all want very much to understand what in heaven's name is going on. Please know this, I promised the Lord I would not defend myself against any accusations and I would not attack the other person's character. He told me He would be my vindicator and to just trust Him. I can, however, tell you this."

At that point I shared with the congregation everything that I've already shared with you, the reader, about the deeply missed conference opportunity, my own personal struggles with trusting God in the midst of the discord sown, and my meeting with the evangelist from Scotland and his words to me. When I was finished, I stood there at the pulpit to a room of silence. Suddenly a couple in the back of the room stood to their feet and announced, "Pastor, we want you to know that we're on board that ship with you." That moment began a cascade of persons after persons, all standing and pledging their allegiance to stand together with me even though the attacks and lies against my character remained unresolved. By evening's end, the entire church was reunited in strength and trust against this storm of sown discord.

Without sharing a word in my own defense, God had rendered ineffective the attacks of my enemy.

Approximately three weeks later, the man responsible for all this trouble moved out of state with his family.

I learned a valuable lesson that day about God's desire to revisit those times of deeply lost opportunities in our life. Sometimes God will revisit such times to bring that exact opportunity to fulfillment and satisfaction just as it was originally presented. It's an awesome thing to see God do that in the midst of something that seems irretrievably lost. It is never wrong to believe God will work that way on our behalf; in fact, very frequently, He will do just that. But I've also learned to not hold on to that expectation so tightly that it blinds us to the possibilities that God may want to work something on our behalf of far greater significance than we could have envisioned. In my case, instead of a three-day conference, I acquired a deeper sense of trust in God. The trust factor in all of this is capable of sustaining one for a lifetime against the storms of life, while a conference would have been but a brief stop along the road to refresh in that moment.

Don't let your disappointment over a deeply lost opportunity keep you blinded to God's desire to revisit such moments with something of far greater consequence to your life. When we dwell on our deep disappointment over what we didn't receive, it has the capability of masking from us the deeper things He wants us to receive.

We serve a God who loves to bless us with the desires of our heart, but when those desires aren't forthcoming the exact way we envision them, we feel deeply jilted at times. We need to be able to learn to trust the one who never jilts and loves to bless. He is the one who proclaims, *"For I know the plans I have for you. They are plans for good and not for disaster, to give you a future and a hope."* (Jeremiah 29:11)

Five

REVISITING DEEP HOPELESSNESS

He sat under a solitary broom tree and prayed that he might die. "I have had enough, Lord," he said. "Take my life, for I am no better than my ancestors who have already died."

1 Kings 19:4 (New Living Translation)

The prophet, Elijah, had just experienced an incredibly spiritual victory for Israel. In a spiritual showdown with King Ahab and hundreds of his false prophets, he had single-handedly brought the nation of Israel to a recommitment of their lives to the one true God. It had been a day of great display of God's power as He manifested Himself as a consuming fire, proving Himself to be who Elijah claimed Him to be when tested against the false gods of Ahab. At the end of the day, Elijah put a cap on the day's events by beheading the assembled false prophets.

The very next day, Ahab's queen, Jezebel, threatened to do to Elijah what he had done to her false prophets. Whether Elijah was totally fatigued or he had just let his guard down, we are not told in the scripture. All we are told is that in deep hopelessness and depression, Elijah, feeling all alone, ran for his life, crying out that he wanted to die. Fortunately, God revisited Elijah, by manifesting Himself to the distraught prophet and reassuring Elijah that there were 7,000 others in the land who, like himself, had not bowed the knee to any false gods.

God is always faithful to His faithful servants. He will neither leave them nor forsake them. When life's circumstances seem overwhelming and hopelessness seeks to take control, He loves to revisit and restore the one sinking in despair.

I believe that, like most believers, pastors sometimes hit "dry spells" in the walk of service with the

Lord. They are those times where, for whatever reason, we struggle to keep a right perspective and find ourselves slipping into deep hopelessness. We are our own worst enemies during such times. I don't believe it reveals a flawed character but rather an area weak in trust and faith that God might strengthen and bring us up higher than before we succumbed to this deep place.

Most of us, if we are honest, probably can remember resigning from going on with the Lord, vowing, "If this is what it's like, well… I didn't sign up for this." If we pull away, we usually succumb to feeling like somehow we've failed the Lord, and we spiral downward into deep hopelessness.

I remember such a time. What I can't recall is the circumstance that led me to finding myself in a state of deep hopelessness and depression. It was an awful time of personal struggle; I wanted to just give up and run away. These feelings coincided with our pastor's annual conference in Billings, Montana. While it wasn't mandatory that we attend with our spouses, it was expected. For Judith Ellen and I, going meant that I would have to attend alone; we still had two small children that needed her at home. Blanketed in deep hopelessness, I had already decided that the annual conference was the last place in the world I wanted to attend or even consider, especially alone.

As the date approached, my wife, sensing that my reluctance to attend the conference would only be more detrimental to my well-being, began earnestly encouraging me to go. I resisted for as long as I could, but she prevailed, convincing me that God would have something for me if I went. I reluctantly agreed to attend but, in all truthfulness, my heart was not in it at all.

As I begrudgingly packed my bag, she slipped into the room and put both her arms around me, seeking to somehow encourage me that everything would be alright. She smiled and said, "Remember your life verse that God gave you. It's so important."

At that point God had given me Hebrews 10:23 as a verse of scripture to "camp on" for the several years. It stated: *Hold fast the confession of your hope, without wavering, because He who promised is faithful.*

"Yeah, yeah," I snapped back, not wanting to be reminded of this verse of hope.

I eventually was ready to go, and as I was getting in the car, Judith Ellen was standing in the front door, smiling and waving. "Don't forget your life verse, sweetie," she shouted. I gave her a forced smile and wave and pulled out of the driveway.

It was a long four-and-a-half-hour trip to Billings, made all the longer by my deep sourness. Awash in my hopelessness, I just wanted to be left alone; an uplifting spiritual conference was the furthest thing from my mind. I was even angry with myself that I had let my wife talk me into going.

When I finally arrived at the motel where I would be staying, I walked into the lobby to the reception desk. It was a beautiful place with well over a hundred rooms. As I neared the desk, my eyes were drawn to a message marquee above it. Emblazoned across the board were the words in bright colors: "Welcome Guest of the Day – Charlie Moody." I stopped in my tracks, immediately thinking, *Great, Judith Ellen's called ahead and had them put this up to make me feel better.*

"Can I help you?" asked the smiling desk clerk.

"Yeah, I'm checking in. I have a reservation."

"Name please?" queried the clerk.

"Sure, Moody, Charlie Moody."

"Mr. Moody. We've been expecting you."

"I'll bet you have," I snapped back. "So what's with my name on the marquee? Did my wife call and ask that it be done?"

"Oh, no, Mister Moody. It's a curtesy that we extend to one of our guests every day. Our computer randomly picks a guest each day, and today your name was picked." She smiled, handing me my registration form and room key. "Oh, one more thing, your complimentary gift basket is in your room. Thanks for choosing us for your stay."

When I entered the room, sitting on the table was a basket filled with fruits and snacks and beverages. It was truly a beautiful gift basket. Immediately, I called Judith Ellen to let her know I arrived safely.

"By the way, you won't believe what happened." I proceeded to tell her about the marquee and the complimentary basket.

She replied, gleefully, "See, everything is going to be alright. God's blessing you. He wants you to know He cares and is with you."

I'm sure I rolled my eyes, preferring to not abandon my disposition to the possibility of the Lord's working on my behalf.

"Oh, before you go, I want to remind you, don't forget your life verse, honey. *Hebrews 10:23, Hold fast the confession of your hope without wavering because He who promised is faithful.* He loves you so much, honey." Her words dripped with reassurance.

"Thanks. Well, I had better go and get ready for tonight's session. I love you; talk with you later."

"Love you, too. Have a good time."

As I prepared for the evening ahead, I couldn't refrain from mulling over the sense that something truly was at work in my hopelessness, but I still wasn't ready to relinquish wallowing in my hopeless feelings just yet.

Arriving late, just as the conference was starting, I sat as far in the back as I could so I would not have to engage anyone in conversation. The room was filled with at least 50 other pastors, many with their spouses. Praise and worship began and was followed by our district superintendent welcoming all of us. After a brief word concerning the theme of the conference, he was ready to introduce the keynote speaker.

"It's with great pleasure that we welcome Cliff Hanes. I know we'll all be blessed by what he brings from the Lord. Let's all give a warm welcome to Cliff."

Everyone stood and applauded as Cliff walked across the platform to the podium. When he finally stood behind the podium, everyone sat, eager to hear this well-recognized and gifted speaker.

"Thank you very much. It's a great honor to be here with the Yellowstone District for your annual conference."

He stopped, looked down at his notes, and got silently reflective.

Finally, looking up, after what seemed like an inordinately long time, he said, "This is a bit unusual. I have these notes that the Lord gave me for tonight's message, but as I walked to the pulpit, I felt that the Lord wanted me to lay these aside and bring something else forth tonight. I believe that what He's put on my heart is truly for someone here tonight. So, if you would, please open your bibles to Hebrews 10:23, *Hold fast the confession of your hope without wavering because He who promised is faithful.*"

Unrestrained tears began to flow. A sudden realization broke through my demeanor that Jesus cared enough to orchestrate an entire change to the evening's venue just for me. I was undone as a sense of love's reassuring warmth washed me in His embrace as deep hopelessness gave way to a restored sense of purpose and unhindered destiny. I later left the conference totally set free from the deep hopelessness that had so tightly gripped me.

Be assured, God has not left you to languish in hopelessness or depression. Remember, He is the one who proclaims over your life in Him, *"I will never leave you alone, never! And I will not loosen My grip on your life"* (Hebrews 13:5 *The Passion Translation*). When we find ourselves caught up in circumstances and situations that leave us vulnerable to influences of hopelessness and depression, it is often difficult to believe that the Lord is still there in the midst of it all with us. Remember, it doesn't depend on you to turn things around, it depends on the One who loves you without measure. He is ever faithful to do just that. We have but to cry out and He loves to show Himself in hope afresh by revisiting you when you are least able to see Him in your pain.

I don't want to minimize or trivialize what you might be going through. I truly know how painful it can be, but I also have come to know how "over the top" His love and care for us are as well. My life verse, at that time in my life, said "to hold on to the *confession* of hope…" Sometimes that's all we have… a verbal agreement to a hope we can not feel. Trust me, with the Lord, it is enough.

Ask the Lord for a life verse of scripture for the season of life you find yourself in. Often it is custom fit for your level of growth with the Lord. It's not unusual to get different life verses for varying seasons of your life with Him. We grow and change; what pertains today may not be relevant tomorrow. Life verses have the capability of calling forth a revisit from the Lord into a deep need within.

It is during these times that we also have a tendency to withdraw from others, being overwhelmed with the weightiness of our emotional state. As much as it's possible, realize that's when we most need the encouragement and support of others. It's not unusual for the Lord to revisit you through the loving kindness and care of others. My wife was an unfailing ally and hand of the Lord, through whom He was constantly revisiting me in my deep hopeless state.

Six

REVISITING WHAT DEEPLY MATTERS MOST

And I will give you a new heart, and I will put a new spirit in you. I will take out your stony stubborn heart and give you a tender, responsive heart.

Ezekiel 36:26 (New Living Translation)

Sometime early in our walk with the Lord, before we went into full-time ministry as pastors, we served on the church board where we attended. We were both still relatively new in our Christianity, yet exhibited enough passion to be considered for the board opportunity. Passion, as I have come to realize, is not always synonymous with maturity.

It was during this period of time that two events happened simultaneously which would forever alter my perception of the Lord and His love. While on the church board, a strong dissension erupted in our midst. The pastor had inadvertently done something that caused a rift and marked division among us. Every meeting during that time ended in harsh disagreement between the board members. Bit by bit, I found myself being drawn more deeply into choosing a side. The consequence was that a deep bitterness overshadowed my heart.

It was during this same period that I began to develop a small, painful lump in my groin area. Every day I would pray for a supernatural healing to occur. The lump only continued to grow in size and discomfort. At its worst, it grew to a lump the size of half a golf ball. Fearing that it might be cancerous, I chose to exercise denial rather than faith. I continued to pray, but between the unchanging lump and the encroaching bitterness, I grew steadily discouraged.

Finally in frustration and anger I cried out to God, "Why won't You heal me? I know healing can come from You, but You choose to ignore me."

In that moment, the most extraordinary thing happened to me. I'm not one who is prone to visions but suddenly everything before me supernaturally faded into a panoramic vision. I was aware that I was standing next to Jesus; His presence was exceptionally strong. I was holding His hand. Suddenly, before my eyes, I saw a young boy some distance away. Just as quickly, I realized that boy was me, and Jesus was allowing me to see how I looked in His eyes. I was repulsed by what I saw. Standing before me was this young boy who was draped in what appeared to be raw sewage. Awareness washed over me that this was how I appeared through Jesus' eyes in all my bitterness.

Immediately, the perception changed and what followed forever changed me in ways that can only be described as glorious. The vision transitioned to my suddenly seeing myself through Jesus' heart. Gone was the sewage slime, replaced by an all-consuming brilliant white light of His love. It was a light brighter than anything I've seen in the natural world. I was blinded to everything else but this light. As it grew in intensity, I felt myself engulfed in a love like I've never experienced. I felt myself being absorbed in this love. It was overwhelming; so overwhelming that I found myself crying out, "Enough!" I feared that if I continued to surrender to this intense light and love I would literally cease to exist, being caught up into His presence forever.

In Genesis 5:24, the Living Translation tells us that Enoch walked in close fellowship with God. Then one day he disappeared... Based on my experience that day, I believe I understand what happened to him. Instantly, I was back in the natural, weeping uncontrollably, crying out for God to forgive me for my sin of bitterness.

This was the most defining moment in my life as a believer. For years I was unable to recount this experience without being tearfully overwhelmed at the scope of God's love toward us, even in our most vile moments. As a pastor, it forever changed my perception of everyone who would enter our fellowship as having inestimable value to the Lord and His Kingdom.

God wasn't done with me yet that day. At that particular time in my life I was not yet a pastor; I worked as a lineman for a cable TV company. After every work order of that day, the entire experience with the

Lord and His love for me while even in my bitterness would be replayed before I arrived at my next work order. By the end of the day I was totally undone and exhausted physically, emotionally, and spiritually.

When I arrived home that evening, Judith Ellen took one look at me and said with great concern, "Are you okay? You don't look well." Not wanting to engage in conversation, I only explained that it had been a hard day and I was exhausted. I excused myself, telling her that I was going to go upstairs and shower for our church board meeting that night.

I went upstairs, stripped down and went into the bathroom. I stood at the sink and looked into the mirror. Immediately the entire vision experience again played out before me as I stood there. I dropped to my knees and bawled, repenting in genuine sorrow over the deep bitterness that racked my heart. His love in my failure was more than I could stand. At some point in all of this, Judith Ellen had come upstairs to check on me.

At that moment, I heard a voice in my heart telling me to stand up. Laboriously, I got to my feet. The voice then commanded me to look down at my groin area. The lump that had previously been so painful had been forgotten amidst the day's events. Before our eyes, we watched as an invisible scalpel sliced a painless vertical incision into the tumor. There was no blood as the incision spread apart, allowing a two to three inch piece of wood to emerge from inside the tumor.

Years earlier, I had a life-threatening industrial accident where I fell 20 feet off a telephone pole, becoming impaled on a fencepost. After extensive reconstructive surgery, I was now viewing a miracle extraction of a piece of wood that had been left inside of me.

The piece of wood emerged only half way. The voice instructed me again to reach down and take the piece of wood out the rest of the way myself. I did, and as I held the piece of wood between my fingers, we watched the incision close itself miraculously without scarring as the tumor then disappeared.

We both fell into each other's arms, weeping at God's goodness. In that one day, I was completely set free from the deep bitterness that bound my heart and I was simultaneously healed of a painful tumor. I stood there, holding the piece of wood, suddenly recognizing the fact that my physical healing was directly correlated to my spiritual healing.

I wrapped the wood in a piece of tissue and left it on my bureau because we had to get ready for that evening's board meeting. I can't say I was looking forward to the meeting after such a glorious breakthrough that day.

We arrived on time, went through the preliminaries of prayer, minutes, and the financial report, and proceeded to the business portion of the meeting. It wasn't very long before the same bickering and disgruntled attitudes reemerged. With each passing minute the tension escalated until board members were snapping in anger at each other. Judith Ellen and I could not enter into the turmoil after what we had just experienced. I sat there in silence, watching the unfolding discord. Finally, one of the board members, provoked by my silence, turned on me.

"What's the matter with you? Don't you have anything to say about all this?"

A cessation of bickering occurred in that moment as the board waited for my response. I looked around the table, and all I could say was, "Sorry, but I don't have anything to say about any of these issues. Honestly, all I can say is this." At that moment, I began to recant the awesome events of that day. When I was finished, there was a silence in the room that was striking. I watched as one board member after another looked around the room at the other board members. Then without provocation, board member after board member arose and went to each other asking forgiveness for their attitude. Weeping and forgiveness broke the stronghold of disagreement through all the Lord did that day. Unity was restored, and God was glorified. What mattered most deeply to the heart of God had been revisited with reconciliation and healing.

And upon arriving home later that evening, I proceeded to retrieve the wood fragment wrapped in tissue, but it was nowhere to be found. Both my wife and I looked extensively for it. No windows had been left open. The only conclusion we could come to was that the Lord removed it so that He might be venerated as my healer and the wood would not become an idol of distraction.

God absolutely loves to revisit those areas that matter most to His heart when we stray from them in favor of something of lesser importance. The reason such areas matter the most to His heart is because we matter most of all to Him. His genuine desire is that we would walk this life with His best, not His least. He remains always the God of "Never the Less" but "Always the More." He revisits those places to remind us not to settle for the less but always remember to have an expectation for His best. John 10:10 (New Jewish Translation) says it best: *I have come that you might have life and that life in its fullest measure.*

Seven

REVISITING DEEPLY LOST LIFE UPGRADES

"Why are you crying, Hannah?" Elkanah would ask. "Why aren't you eating? Why be downhearted just because you have no children?

When Elkanah slept with Hannah, the Lord remembered her plea, and in due time she gave birth to a son. She named him Samuel, for she said, "I asked the Lord for him."

1 Samuel 1:8, 19-20 (New Living Translation)

Hannah lived in a time where having children was a recognized sign of God's granted favor and blessings upon one's status. Not having children was considered degrading to a married woman. Hannah found herself in just such a place. She found herself crying out in great intercession that she might become more than just a wife; she wanted desperately to become a mother.

The Lord heard her cries and revisited her barrenness, granting her an upgrade in status, the birth of a baby boy. The upgrade was bigger than she or anyone else could have imagined. Hannah gave birth to the prophet Samuel, one of Israel's greatest prophets.

Life, for most of us, is a continuous series of life upgrades. We graduate to bigger education opportunities as we grow older. In employment, we find ourselves being remunerated with pay increases if we prove ourselves an asset, sometimes even being promoted to higher-up positions. Many move from being single to being married and building a family. In short, upgrades come to most of us throughout our lives.

In my life of ministry, I've never considered it essential or important to be ordained. I know that goes against the norm, but I was totally content to only be a licensed minister. In my mind, I was in good company; Charles Spurgeon and D.L. Moody were never ordained and look at what they accomplished for the Kingdom of God. Please understand, my primary reason for not being ordained was not based on their choice, but it helped me feel more at peace with my decision.

For my first 28 years of pastoral ministry, I never felt a need for a ministry upgrade from licensing to ordination. All that changed when our denomination decided that my wife (who was also licensed) and I, plus a myriad of other pastors would receive ordination. It was their reasoning that every pastor who had served long enough and proved themselves faithful to the call should not have to "jump through any more hoops" to receive this upgrade. We both qualified and were invited to join many other pastors at an upcoming Foursquare Gospel conference to have ordination bestowed upon us.

Even though my wife and I had never actually sought ordination, we decided that we would avail ourselves of the freely offered opportunity. We formally accepted the invitation to receive our ordination at our next divisional conference, an annual three-day meeting of approximately 75 pastors and families for the purpose of encouragement and yearly business. Even though we had never entertained the idea of being ordained as a necessity for our ministry, we found ourselves actually excited about the upcoming event.

In the interim between accepting the invitation and going were several months of daily ministry duties that, as always, kept us both occupied and busy. One ministry need that arose at that time was to a person of our congregation who was diagnosed with terminal cancer. We committed ourselves to his spiritual comforting and assurance. Continual visitations and meals became the norm. Over time, however, his declining health demanded more around-the-clock attention. He was moved to a long-term care facility where he could be more closely monitored and helped. We continued visiting him regularly. The day before we were to leave for our ordination, we stopped to see him and let him know that we wouldn't be available for several days.

Finally the day to leave for the conference came. We had gone from nonchalance toward ordination to now eagerly looking forward to the event. With great anticipation we left for the conference, knowing that our denomination was pulling out all stops to make this a momentous occasion.

We drove the three and half hours to the conference site, arriving about an hour before the ordination service was to begin. It was exciting to reconnect with so many ministry friends that we only saw rarely. The very air of the conference center buzzed with anticipation for what was about to occur.

Then it happened.

Just before we were about to enter the sanctuary of the church where this wonderfully honoring event was to take place, our cell phone rang. We answered it to hear the frantic voice of one our hometown congregants declare, "I just wanted you both to know that Richard has taken a sudden turn for the worse and is not expected to last the night."

We thanked her for the phone call, hung up, and looked at each other in disbelief. There was no question as to our next move. We sought the administrators of the conference, explaining why we couldn't stay. They assured us that there would be some other opportunity, somewhere down the road. We walked out of the church as people were filtering into the sanctuary to the beginning sounds of the praise and worship team.

Now I would love to be able to say at this point that my heart was totally noble in commitment to show up as Richard's "spiritual white knight," riding into his room just in the nick of time before he passed. I would like to say that, but honestly, I spent most of the return home wrestling with my genuine love and care for Richard and my feelings of being deeply thwarted from receiving what would now be considered to me a life in ministry upgrade.

By the time we arrived at the care center, it was well after midnight, and I had come to the place of being settled with the knowledge that I had gone all those preceding years without ordination and that I would just go forward as though nothing had changed.

We braced ourselves as we approached Richard's room for what we knew would probably be a somber time. We wondered if we were in time. As we entered the room, we were met with a scene that shocked us. Sitting up in bed was Richard, a coke in one hand and a book in the other.

"Hey guys," he beamed gleefully, pulling himself up into a better sitting position, readying himself to visit.

"How's it goin'? Back so soon?" He smiled brightly.

"Richard," I said as I walked across the room toward his bed, "Someone called us and said you weren't going to make it through the night!"

"Well, I wondered earlier this evening, but I'm fine now," he said confidently.

I'm sure I must have looked at Judith Ellen with a blank disbelief. An invisible silent shrug passed between us as the total realization of what had just occurred washed over us both. I only vaguely remember what we said in those moments after arriving at Richard's beside; the deep sense of our lost ministry upgrade blanketed our minds and hearts.

At some point we left Richard, exhausted and drained, as we headed home for some much-needed rest.

In the days and weeks that followed, we resigned ourselves to our disappointment, choosing instead to immerse ourselves in ministry work.

Then one Sunday, at the beginning of services, a couple from our fellowship came to the front of the church. With great formality they stated, "Pastor Charlie and Pastor Judith Ellen, we all realize that you both had to forgo a special opportunity to be blessed in your ministry with ordination. First of all, we want to recognize your unselfishness and caring love as our pastors. Secondly, while you both may not have received a formal certification of ordination, we want to assure you that we recognize you as already being worthy of that honor. And so we want to present you with this informal certification, signed lovingly by us all, acknowledging you before God and us as already ordained."

They then presented us with a handmade certificate, stating our ordination. It was dated and signed by everyone in the fellowship. We were deeply touched by their love. No formal certification could have ever meant as much to us as the handmade one that our church had bestowed upon us.

But God wasn't done.

Several weeks later, we received a phone call from our district leadership. They shared that they had discovered that our loss of ordination was because of our willingness to put the needs of another before our opportunity. Consequently, it was decided that they would come to our church for the following Sunday's service to conduct an ordination service for both of us before our congregation. They shared that this was something that had never been done in the history of our denomination; ordination had always been done in conference settings.

The following Sunday, two administrators came and conducted an ordination service. It was a tremendous celebration of a deeply missed life upgrade fully restored. We were, in fact, ordained twice in the same denomination, an event I've never heard of happening for anyone in ministry.

In Psalm 43:5, the psalmist to not be discouraged or disturbed but rather have a full expectation of a divine breakthrough for whatever might be the cause of that deep disappointment. I've had several computers over the years that have succumbed to operating system upgrades. What occurred, in essence, was with continual upgrades, the computer eventually reached a point in its life where it no longer could support receiving the newer state of the upgrades. In some instances, the older operating system was completely replaced by a more advanced, incompatible program for the old computer. I had to either buy a newer computer or limp along with an older system, which sometimes was no longer technically supported.

Our heavenly Father loves to bring upgrades to our life. He says in Isaiah 43:19, "*I am doing something brand new, something unheard of. Even now it sprouts and grows and matures. Don't you perceive it?*" The life you live in Christ Jesus was made for divine upgrades. You don't need to get a new operating system, you already have the only one you will ever need (2 Corinthians 5:17), and God is constantly upgrading us to greater realizations of our true nature as His children. Here is the good news: With each upgrade, your life continually gets better; you do not need another new life, you only need to receive the upgrades when they come. He is faithful to render upgrades into your life. Our deep disappointments concerning life's upgrades that seemingly don't come have nothing to do with God's unwillingness. If it is truly His will, it will come. Most often it is the way and timing of our expectation for these things to occur that creates the deep discouragement. Fix your eyes on Him, wait upon His timing, and do not allow deep discouragement to keep you from the joy of His life upgrades.

Remember, in Jesus, you are not now who you were five years ago, you've grown (an upgrade). And five years from now, you will not be who you are today. Life in the Kingdom is never stagnation, it is always awakening to newer and better upgrades.

Eight

RE-VISITATIONS

... I do have one compelling focus: I forget all of the past as I fasten my heart to the future instead.

Philippians 3:13 (The Passion Translation)

"For I know the plans I have for you," says the Lord. "They are plans for good and not for disaster, to give you a future and a hope."

Jeramiah 29:11 (The New Living Translation)

As evidenced by both these scriptures, God wants us as believers to not be bound by our history but to live in light of our destiny. Every believer's destiny has key elements that are uniquely the individual's; there are locations, there are spiritual gifts, there are ministries, etc. No two destinies are completely the same except for one area. The ultimate goal of every believer's destiny finds its true meaning not in what we end up doing but in whose likeness we end up becoming: Christ-like. That is the one element that is the same for every believer's destiny.

For he knew all about us before we were born and he destined us from the beginning to share the likeness of his Son.

Romans 8:29 (The Passion Translation)

Becoming Christ-like isn't just God's desire for us, but it is the ultimate purpose for salvation. Everything else is but a byproduct – a glorious byproduct – but a byproduct nonetheless. Salvation takes us out of a kingdom of darkness and into a kingdom of light, assuring an eternal home in heaven. This, however, is but an end goal to the process of living out one's destiny.

Knowing that everyone has a destiny from the Lord in this life truly adds meaning and purpose. Genuine fulfillment comes when we are able to successfully know our destiny and see it fulfilled. This is the Lord's desire for us as well.

I have come that you might have life, life in its fullest measure.

John 10:10 (The Jewish New Testament)

There are, however, deeply experienced events and circumstances which happen in everyone's life that can set up "stumbling blocks" to progressing in our destiny. In the previous seven chapters, I've shared some of my own personal "deep blockages" that needed to be revisited and overcome.

The purpose of this book is not intended to identify every "deep" place of struggle that others go through. Rather, it is written that there might be an emerging sense of understanding and hope for all who recognize the reality of such personal difficulties. You are not the sum of all your pre-Jesus experiences as much as you are now the sum of all He is and what He declares you to be.

The deep places of personal struggles are very real. Yet, like Simon in Luke 5, when revisited with Jesus, they can become places and events of great breakthrough and blessing. For Simon, it became a defining moment for literally stepping into his divinely ordained destiny. I've attempted to validate that reality in all my shared testimonies. Each one was experienced in the light of bringing me more fully into the knowledge and anointing of my purpose in Christ Jesus. He wants the same for you.

> *For your fleeting life is but a warm breath of air that is visible in the cold only for a moment and then vanishes!*

James 4:14 (The Passion Translation)

Living in Montana means dealing with harsh winter temperatures, often subzero. Years ago, it was one such day that registered -30 degrees without wind. A friend wanted to demonstrate the severity of such cold. He proceeded to take a cup of boiling water and throw the water into the -30-degree air. The water never fell to the ground but instantly became a vaporous cloud which drifted off into the frigid air.

In the span of eternity, that is what your life and mine look like; here today, gone tomorrow. That being said, we need to understand that the brevity of life needs to be lived as fully as possible. We serve a God who lives outside the confinement of time. He told Moses to tell the children of Israel that His name is, "I Am", not "I Was" or "I Shall Be," but "I Am" (*Exodus 3:14*). Our God who lives always without beginning or end declares over us that He has plans for us in this short span of time to know hope and a future (*Jeremiah 29:11*). He does not desire to see us, His children, weighed down from accomplishing His plans for us by unresolved deep obstructions in our lives.

He wants us to succeed more than we do. And there is not one thing He will not do to see those plans He has for you come to fruition. We must not allow the nature of our deep personal issues to become that which defines us according to limitations. Instead, we must stand in the promises of the one who will never fail us.

So now we must cling tightly to the hope that lives within us, knowing that God always keeps his promises.

Hebrews 10:23 (The Passion Translation)

Nine

DEEP INTIMACY

And by his one perfect sacrifice he made us perfectly holy and complete for all time!

Hebrews 10:14 (The Passion Translation)

Sometimes the deep struggles of our lives tend to skew the truth of what God has said and accomplished on our behalf. This is why it is so essential that God's children become a people of His word. I realize many believers would say that they are always in the word yet still face unresolved struggles with deep issues in their lives. What we often fail to understand is that as necessary as it is to be in the word, it is more important that we get the word in us. This is God's love letter to believers. 2 Timothy 3:16 tells us that "all scripture is inspired by God." This means literally that it is breathed with the essence of who God is.

One thing I have always sought to do over the course of my marriage is to leave little notes to my wife in obvious places expressing my love to her. Romancing is an essential ingredient to a successful marriage. God's word is His love notes to us, expressing who He is and how He feels toward us. It is always easier to trust someone who is so transparent about their reckless abandonment of love toward us. God is a reckless lover.

Over my 30-plus years in ministry, the Lord has had me remind our fellowship several times a year to always be a people of the word and a people of prayer. It might seem silly to have to tell believers that over and over, but it is necessary because many do not have a prayer life or a consistency of time spent with God's word. Both of these elements are crucial for break-throughs in the deep issues of one's life. How can one stand on His promises if His promises are absent from the heart? How can one hear and know the love and care of our heavenly Father if we never spend time communicating to Him and allowing Him to speak His reassurances and promises to us? All of this sounds like basic stuff because it is. Famous Green Bay Packer coach Vince Lombardi never took the game or his players for granted. It did not matter how many seasons or how few the players had been around, he always started the new season with the most foundational statement that could be made. Holding a football in his hand, he would stand before his assembled players and declare, "Gentlemen, this is a football."

One day Jesus taught the apostles to keep praying and never stop or lose hope.

Luke 18:1 (The Passion Translation)

For the believer, prayer is an essential self-discipline. I realize that the word "self-discipline" conjures up visions of harsh, demanding, personal structure to one's life. While there is an element of truth to that, it is not necessary that self-discipline be harsh or demanding but rather that it be habitual. We need to make it a habit to take a special part of our day to spend with the one who loves to be with us.

"On judgment day many will say to me, 'Lord! Lord! We prophesied in your name and cast out demons in your name and performed many miracles in your name.' But I will reply, 'I never knew you. Get away from me, you who break God's laws.'"

Matthew 7:22-23 (New Living Translation)

Jesus is making an important statement here regarding the priorities that He values most in His relationship with us. The word "knew" used by Jesus is a term of intimacy most often used in scripture referring to the intimacy of a married couple. In essence, what Jesus is declaring is that while He values the things we do for Him, He is more desirous of those things emanating out of our intimate times spent with Him.

Find a place and time that is special and works for taking those moments to spend in communication with the Lord. Make it personal, fitting to what works best for you being able to formulate this time together. For me, four o'clock in the morning works best. I am an early riser, and I chose this time when we were raising our children. This time was early enough that I was undisturbed in my time with Him. I found if I waited until later in the day I never seemed to get that time back; the tyranny of daily business would see to that. Our kids are now adults, living on their own, raising families as well, but the prayer time for me has remained the same. It just works for me and Jesus. Four o'clock in the morning may seem extreme to most, so find what works best for you; it's all good with Him.

He will never slumber or sleep...

Psalm 121:4 (The Passion Translation)

Another aspect of prayer that is so important to the relationship is to develop a spiritual ear to hear. All too often, believers spend all of their prayer time laying out their "lists" of things that are on their heart. The Lord wants to hear from you, but He also wants to share His heart with you.

"And the sheep recognize the voice of the true Shepard, for he calls his own by name and leads them out...

John 10:3 (The Passion Translation)

Note: Jesus is not saying that believers might hear His voice, He is saying that they do hear His voice! I have met so many Christians over the years that say they do not hear the Lord at all. In most instances, it is purely a matter of training the heart to hear. Learn to sit quietly as part of your prayer time learning to hear. We spend so little time tuning our spiritual ears to hear, that it may take time to develop this critically important aspect of prayer. Be patient, it will come. When this happens (and it will), then it is time to listen.

"Anyone with ears to hear should listen and understand."

Matthew 11:15 (New Living Translation)

A wise man will listen and add to his wisdom...

Proverbs 1:5 (Aramaic Bible in Plain English)

The Lord has a multitude of ways to communicate with us. It might be an audible voice or a seemingly random thought that leaves one questioning, *"Where did that come from?"* Or it can come through visions and dreams. Again, training ourselves to both hear and listen to the Lord is a vital part of intimacy in a relationship.

One other method that God uses to communicate is through His inspired word: the Bible. As already stated, this "inspired" aspect of God's word carries the meaning that it is literally "breathed with the essence" of who God is. Jesus, speaking to the Jewish leaders, said in John 5:39, "You search the scriptures because you think they give you eternal life. But the scriptures point to me!" (New Living Translation)

I spend time every day in His Word. I read according to an outline purposed to take me through the entire Bible in one year. There is almost always a journal that I keep nearby to write down any thoughts and revelations I might sense as being from God concerning each days reading. Over the years, I have amassed volumes filled with divine inspiration and revelation. God speaks through His word.

Get a translation that works for you. When I was a new believer, I was led by a wonderful woman who owned a Christian bookstore to a contemporary, easy-to-read version. There are well-intentioned believers who will tell you that only this or that version is acceptable. As long as it is not a bible translated by a cult-like religion, it's usually safe. I find that the Holy Spirit is more concerned with being understood than He is extremely troubled by translations. I currently draw from and cross reference among as many as 30 various translations.

The Lord, who so loves manifesting Himself in us and through us to render freedom and release from the deep captivating issues of our lives, does so most proficiently through our time together with Him. Prayer and the word are key to such togetherness. As evidenced from Simon in Luke 5, being close to Jesus and hearing and listening to what He says brings great breakthroughs for our deep issues. Practicing these essentials bring healing and deliverance.

Ten

DEEPLY BELOVED

This is love: He loved us long before we loved him. It was his love, not ours. He proved it by sending his Son to be the pleasing sacrificial offering to take away our sins.

1 John 4:10 (The Passion Translation)

Let me say right up front: You, dear reader, are God's favorite. This is how He genuinely thinks and feels about you. If you were the only person on the planet, Father God would have sent His Son just for you. Your value to Him and His Kingdom is inestimable. The amazing thing is that He feels the same way about all His children. Each and every one of us is His favorite. It could be easily said that our God is an equal-opportunity lover. It is not that He loves one more than another, it's that He loves equally.

Ex-heavyweight boxer George Forman named all five of his sons George. It has always been considered strange and quirky by most; George himself has even jokingly made lighthearted comments about it. The real reason that he did it was because he grew up never knowing who his own father was. So he decided that when he was married and had children, they would grow up always knowing who their father was. Hence they were all named George.

Our heavenly Father didn't make us all the same that we might come to know Him by some uniform standard, but gave us His Son, that we, in Jesus, might now know our Father by and through Jesus.

My old identity has been crucified with Messiah and no longer lives; for the nails of his cross crucified me with him. And now the essence of this new life is no longer mine, for the Anointed One lives his life through me – we live in union as one! My new life

*is empowered by the faith of the Son of God
who loves me so much that He gave Himself
for me, and dispenses His life in to mine.*

Galatians 2:20 (The Passion Translation)

The Father does not see you with any bias or hierarchy; He sees you in Christ Jesus His Son.

In Luke 15:11-31, Jesus tells an illustrated story about the relationship of a loving father and his two sons. One lived in total worldliness, squandering all his family inheritance blessings. He eventually returns home filled with remorse and an overwhelming sense of unworthiness. The other son stayed close to home, working diligently in the family business. He felt overlooked and unappreciated for his faithfulness. Both sons did not understand the love that their father had for them. In the story, both sons experience the same unfailing love of the father. Neither one was loved more or less than the other, but equally according to their need. It is a marvelous illustration of our Father's love toward us.

It is so important that you and I realize how loved we truly are because when we truly know this in our heart, we begin to appreciate that there is no deep place in our lives that isn't important to our God. And there is not any personal issue so deep that He can't and won't heal, restore, or deliver us from.

The first seven years of my ministry in Libby, Montana was focused almost completely on the theme of "who we are in Christ." The Holy Spirit would not let me depart from this message. In one form or another, this was the basic direction to everything we did as a church. As a body of believers, we all came to appreciate this because it strongly made us aware of our Father's unwavering love and goodness toward us. To know this as truth is to know unequivocally His willingness to revisit with us the deep, unresolved areas of our lives. We have to apprehend the knowledge of this truth deep in our hearts if we are to ever move forward into "life in its fullest measure" (John 10:10 The Jewish New Testament). It is hard to fully trust anyone to have your best interests at heart if you don't believe they truly love you.

> *Trust the Lord completely, and do not rely on your own opinions. With all your heart rely on Him to guide you, and He will lead you in every decision you make.*
>
> *Proverbs 3:5 (The Passion Translation)*

In chapter six, I recounted an experience of the all-encompassing, over-the-top love of God for me when I wasn't feeling very lovable. Beside the breakthrough that occurred for me personally, something else emerged from that event as well. No longer could I look at anyone without a total realization of how loved they are by God. It changed me in my relationship to everyone around me, saved and unsaved.

We know how much God loves us, and we have put our trust in His love. God is love, and all who live in love live in God, and God lives in them.

1 John 4:16 (New Living Translation)

Knowing who you are in Christ opens your understanding to the richness of resources that are yours in the Kingdom of God. In 2 Corinthians 5:20, believers are referred to as "ambassadors" of the Lord and His Kingdom. An ambassador represents the country they are from when they are abroad in another country. They have available to them all the resources of the country they represent and the authority to speak on behalf of their homeland. That's what the love of the Father has opened up to you. You now serve His Kingdom, your new home, fully invested with everything of His Kingdom while here on earth. To know this as truth in one's life is to walk in empowerment. You are not the product of your past. To the Father, you are now the product of who you are in Christ Jesus. This means so much when we realize all that the Lord makes available to us as we transition through our deep issues.

Nor height, nor depth (deep areas), nor any other creature shall be able to separate us from the love of God, which is in Christ Jesus our Lord.

Romans 8:39 King James Version) parenthesis mine

You and I are now Christ-likeness to a lost and dying world. Do not let your deep losses, frustrations, detours, and challenges declare who you are.

For he knew all about us before we were born and he destined us from the beginning to share the likeness of his Son. This means the Son is the firstborn among many who will become just like him.

Romans 8:29 (The Passion Translation)

The enemy of our faith, the devil, is an opportunist who would capitalize on the deep issue that you need to be free of to try to convince you that you are not who God, through His word, says you are. It is the original lie back from the beginning. In Genesis, God made man in His image. In other words, Adam and Eve were already like Him. They had only one thing forbidden to them in God's creation – to not eat from the Tree of The Knowledge of Good and Evil. The devil brought doubt to Eve's mind by persuading her to believe that God did not want them to eat of that fruit because He knew that they would then be like Him. Believing the lie, Eve convinced Adam to disobey God with her and eat the fruit. Both believed that God was in some way holding out on them. What they failed to realize was that they did not need to become like God, they were already like Him!

The devil is a defeated foe already, stripped of any power at the cross… except the power to deceive. He still plies this trait quite well, keeping many believers thinking that they are much less than God says they are.

Realizing who you actually are in Christ brings an incredible advantage to your life so that you are less prone to be beneath the circumstances of your deep situation and more on top than you understand.

You are deeply beloved.

Eleven

SEEKING DEEPLY

Lord, when you said to me, "Seek My face," my inner being responded, "I'm seeking Your face with all my heart."

Psalm 27:8 (The Passion Translation)

A.W. Tozer, stated so appropriately in his book *The Pursuit of God: The Human Thirst for The Divine*: "Why do some persons 'find' God in a way that others do not? Why does God manifest His presence to some and let multitudes of others struggle along in the half-light of imperfect Christian experience? Of course the will of God is the same for all. He has no favorites within His household. All He has ever done for any of His children He will do for all of His children. The difference lies not with God but with us."

When our two children were three or four, I used to play with them all the time. One of our favorite games was our own version of hide-and-seek. I was always the one who would hide, and they would seek to find me. My hiding places were always extremely obvious and purposed so that I could be found easily. The fun in it all was that when they found me, I would jump out of hiding and begin chasing them as they ran from room to room, shrieking in delight. When I finally caught them, I would fall to the floor and roll around as they would jump on me, laughing and screaming with excitement. It could have easily been said that we were no longer a household with only two children, we had suddenly become three children! Well, scripture says, "Unless you become as little children..." I was practicing.

I've never forgotten those times because they really helped me realize how similar our heavenly Father is with us, His kids. I know that His presence is always with me, but there is a manifest sense of His presence that is most experienced when we pursue and seek Him in the delight and fullness of all that He is.

Bill Johnson in his book, *When Heaven Invades Earth*, makes a statement which I've fully embraced in my walk as a believer. He says, "The church camps around the sermon. Israel camped around the presence. Learning to recognize, treasure and carry His presence is at the heart of the Christian life. Recalibrating our hearts to this supreme value affects everything."

In 1999, several weeks before Thanksgiving, I embarked on a journey that forever changed my perspective and life as a believer regarding the presence of the Lord. That year had been a spiritually dry year in ministry for me. By the beginning of November, I realized that something had to change or I could not continue in ministry. There just seemed to be a disconnect inside, it felt like I was just going through the motions of ministry.

I had heard about a spiritual revival that had been going on for four years. It was called The Brownsville Revival in Pensacola, Florida. All the reports coming from the meetings were truly miraculous. Nightly hundreds attending from all over the world were experiencing life-changing renewal. I made a decision to go there for two weeks in hope of having a restoration of freshness in my ministry. When I left, I told the church, "I feel like Elijah at the Brook Cherith and the brook has dried up and I need to find my Zarephath (1 Kings 17:1-15) or I won't be coming back to ministry."

My hopes were more than met. Nightly, a tangible presence of God would enter into the services, touching and changing lives dramatically. Time and space do not permit me to recount all the powerful miracles of salvations, healings, and deliverances witnessed. Suffice it to say, I count myself among the multitudes that were experiencing the goodness and love of God in the manifestation of His presence. A profound brokenness came into my heart that God was able to take and reformat in complete newness of perception and understanding. I was changed inside. But the most incredible occurrence that happened was that I now knew God in the reality of His manifest presence. Ministry was no longer just about dry, dead religion. It was about a vibrancy of life that flowed through relationship with living presence of God.

That first Sunday back, the glory of His manifest presence came into our service in such a tangible way that it forever changed, not just me, but our entire fellowship.

How important is our pursuit of the presence of God? Well, the following Sunday, everyone came back expecting the same glorious experience of God manifesting Himself in presence and power. That Sunday, however, the same remarkable, tangible sense of His presence was not evident. Oh, He was there but not as we had experienced Him the week prior. You could feel everyone's unspoken questioning, "*What happened?*"

After services, I got home and immediately went to my den. Closing the door behind me, I fell to my knees determined to find out why everything changed from the previous Sunday's experience. Quietly I cried out, "What happened, Lord? Why was everything different this Sunday?" I closed my eyes as I knelt in the silence of the room, hoping I would get an answer. Suddenly, almost imperceptibly, a small voice spoke, "Do you want Me for My presents or do you want me for My Presence?" I was broken by the question. Weeping, I replied in absolute sincerity, "Lord, if I never receive a gift from Your hand again, it is enough to have and know You." A peace washed over me as I realized that everything would now be alright. The following Sunday, the Lord manifested Himself in even greater measure.

You show me the path of life; in Your presence is fullness of joy; at Your right hand are pleasures forevermore.

Psalm 16:11 (New King James Version)

The fullness of joy for our lives, which is declared to be our strength in life (Nehemiah 8:10), is not found in our programs, our presentations, or our platforms. It is found in the abiding manifestation of His presence. All those other things have a genuine place in our services and lives, but they find their fullest meaning and importance if they emanate through His presence.

Truly, His presence is everything.

Moses, in Exodus 33, is told by God that because of the sins of His people, He will not go with them into the Promised Land but send an angel with them instead. Moses, knowing the importance of God above all else says (v.15), "If Your presence does not go with us, do not bring us up from here." He is saying he does not want the Promise without the Promise Giver; he would rather stay in the desert than enter a land for great resources without the presence of God.

In 2 Samuel 6, King David passionately wanted the Ark of the Covenant in Jerusalem where He was. The Ark represented the living presence of God, His glory rested upon it. David would do anything to have the Lord's presence with him. After some missteps in moving the Ark, he finally succeeds. Stripping himself of all his regal apparel, he dances with abandon before the transported Ark, with but a linen undergarment on. When Jerusalem is finally reached, David's wife, Michal, upbraids him for his lack of kingly demeanor. David replies (v. 22), "I will be even more undignified than his, and I will be humble in my own sight." His passion for God's presence outweighed his maintaining royal presentation.

What does this have to do with those "deep troubling waters" of our life? Well, I have come to realize that the greatest joy of being set free from those places and issues comes with the greatest sense of restoration, renewal, refreshing, healing, and deliverance when experienced through the glorious manifestation of the reality of His abiding manifested presence. God can do any of these things just because of who He is and His character. And believe me, it is wonderful to experience His goodness and love on our behalf. In John 9, Jesus heals a man blind from birth. The man knows that it was Jesus who did it, but he did not know the one who did it in manifest presence. It was only later that Jesus reveals Himself to the man in fullness of presence. It says that at that point, an abandonment to worship occurred in the man. There are other such instances in scripture as well.

The Lord can meet you in your "deep issue" without manifesting Himself in presence to render whatever is needed to know total release and freedom. In other words, one can know Him in His power without knowing Him in His Presence. Why not know Him in presence and power? Don't seek just your miracle; seek to know His presence with the miracle. You will be the richer for it.

The Sunday before Thanksgiving, in 1999, when God manifested Himself in presence and power, it was both radical and different than anything we had ever known. The manifestations surrounding His presence were unusual and mighty. People were falling to the floor, slain in the Spirit. Brokenness came upon the hearts of many. One man knelt on the floor cradling the head of one of his five children, all of them slain in the Spirit. All he could do was weep and cry out to anyone near him, "I never knew. I never knew." The order of service that day was His order and it was totally different than anything we had experienced prior. There were those few who left that day, proclaiming, "This couldn't possibly be of God. God would never do such things."

I learned that day not to let personal dignity keep one from His divinity and to not let properness keep one from His presence. I would rather be like King David, dancing in my skivvies and have the fullness of His presence. I don't want His perks without His presence. Simon, in Luke 5, could have experienced the miracle catch of fish without Jesus being in the boat with him, but because Jesus was present with him, there was a depth of realization that transcended the hoard of fish. The presence of Jesus became greater than the fish. Or let's look at it this way, Simon's breakthrough in his place of deep personal frustration was superseded by the manifest presence of the Lord with him!

Yes, God wants to bring personal freedom from your deep struggle but, more importantly, He wants to meet with you in "your boat" at that deep place. Seek Him as you revisit your place in the deep. He loves it when we make the vessel of our lives available to him for a revisitation.

His presence is everything!

This story illustrates this truth: There was an old man who lived with his son who he loved dearly. All they had were each other, there was no other family.

The old man was incredibly wealthy, and over the years, had amassed one of the world's greatest art collections. His acquired art pieces were the envy of the art world. One day, the man's son was drafted into the military; it was a time of war. With great sorrow, the man said goodbye to his son. The months went by, the war continued, and the son was killed in action. The old man's sorrow was inconsolable.

One day, months after his son's death, there was a knock at the door. When the old man opened the door a young man in uniform stood before him. He introduced himself as a close friend of the man's son. They had served together in the war. The young soldier proceeded to produce a rough pencil sketch that he had made of the son and wanted the father to have it. After they had visited a while, the old man excitedly ran into the living room where he moved several works of art from the mantelpiece to prominently display the pencil sketch of his son.

Years went by and the old man eventually passed away. He had left instructions that all his valuable art work was to be auctioned off. The art world buzzed with anticipation at the opportunity to procure these priceless pieces. On the day of the auction art collectors from all over the world showed up for the event. The auctioneer slammed down his gavel; the auction began.

"Our first work is this pencil sketch of the man's son. Do I hear $100?"

Snickers could be heard among the assembled art collectors. A muffled, "*You've got to be kidding!*" was heard.

"Do I hear $50?"

Nothing.

"Do I hear $10?"

An elderly gentleman in the back of the room raised his hand, "I will buy that sketch for $10 dollars. I was the old man's gardener, and I knew and loved both he and his son."

With that sale, the auctioneers gavel fell again, "This auction is now officially over."

Disbelief and hostility erupted from the assembled art collectors, "What do you mean it's over?

Nothing has happened yet except that piece of trash pencil sketch," one man burst out. Murmurs of agreement echoed through the disgruntled collectors.

"Well, it clearly stated in the contract for this sale that *whoever gets the son gets it all!*" announced the auctioneer.

Tan, Paul Lee   *Encyclopedia of 7700 Illustrations* 1979 (p.239)

Whoever gets the Son gets it all.

His presence is worth everything!

Epilogue

This book is in no way intended to be all inclusive on the area of every deep personal need out there. What I believe is the Holy Spirit's intention for putting it on my heart to write this so that others might find renewed hope in a glorious, all-loving God who cares about them more than they ever thought possible. Perhaps reading this has brought a revelation of some deep area that has remained elusive yet its effects have been hindering. Then, hopefully, if nothing else, it at least has triggered the awareness that there is an area that needs to be revisited with the Lord for breakthrough.

More than anything, I want the Lord to be glorified through this and His children to be edified – built up in their journey of faith through this life. I've found over my many years as a believer that so much of whom we are in the Lord and all He intends for us to be is very much an ongoing process of transformation and change.

2 Corinthians 5:17 (The Passion Translation) clearly states: *Now, if anyone is enfolded into Christ, he has become an entirely new creation. All that is related to the old order has vanished. Behold, everything is fresh and new.*

This means by being in Christ Jesus, you are no longer who you used to be. Remember Hebrews 10:14, *By His one perfect sacrifice He has made you perfectly holy and complete for all time (The Passion Translation).*I believe this with all my heart. This truly is how the Lord perceives you. You are already, right now, seated at the right hand of the Father (Ephesians 2:6). That is your new spiritual reality. Yet, so often, our unrenewed minds try to live in contradiction to these truths. A major part of the renewing of the mind to live in accordance with the truth requires replacing the things that hinder correct perception with unwavering reality of truth. Dealing with those deep areas of prior strongholds is a part of the process of wholeness in Christ. Note, I said "process." Ideally, you are already holy and complete but becoming fully that truth, more often than not, is a process of change. The Apostle Paul said in Philippians 4:11, "I have learned to be content regardless of my circumstances" (Berean Study Bible). Even the Apostle Paul is saying that he was in a process of learning to become content, he was not always there. Hear what he also says in Philippians 3:12, "I admit that I haven't yet acquired the absolute fullness that I am pursuing, but I run with passion into His abundance so that I may reach the destiny that Jesus Christ has called me to fulfill and wants me to discover" (The Passion Translation).

I really think what the Holy Spirit wants conveyed in all of this is to not lose heart and hope concerning the deep areas of your life that may still crop up now and then. Be willing to "get in the boat" with Jesus and revisit the deep places of frustration, hurt, loss, unfulfilled dreams, anger, or any other unnamed deep place. With Jesus, it is always worth the journey. He wants to bring renewal, refreshing, and revival to us more than we realize. Recognize, as Simon did, He is the God of "Never the less" because "He is the God of Always the More."

Let us hold fast the confession of our hope without wavering, for He who promised is faithful.

Hebrews 10:23 (New King James Version)

My Prayer for You

Father, I lift up my heart to You today for my brother and sister. Be the God of fresh hope. May they have Your heart fully revealed to them and Your hand ever upon them. Reveal to them even now the unbridled joy that they are to Your heart. You are the Lord of all possibilities; nothing remains elusive from Your touch. Even now, as the deep areas that have been conflicting in the life of my brother and sister in their journey with You begin to resurface and emerge to their understanding, revisit those places with Your healing, loving presence. I declare the unfulfilled dreams from the Lord would be both restored and brought to fruition. May destinies come forth with vibrancy of life. Bless my brother and sister with Your unfailing goodness, Your impassioned love, and Your immeasurable power. Be glorified in their lives. Thank You, Father, for the gift of life and the gift of today.

You may have read this book and wondered about the premise and truth of it all. Perhaps you picked it up out of curiosity or on a friend's recommendation. Maybe you are finding it hard to identify with everything you just read, yet you are now aware of some deep area that has troubled you.

There's hope for you as well and it all starts with a relationship with an all-loving God who wants more than anything to share His life with you now and eternally. This isn't about religion, it's about your relationship with a very caring, loving, and real God. You can know the benefits of everything that has been shared in these pages through merely turning to Him in faith. You see, our sinfulness separates from our God. Sin demands a penalty payment to be erased. You and I, by our very nature, are incapable of being good enough to pay that penalty payment. Jesus on the cross fulfilled that penalty payment for us. Now by faith in what He has done for us, He wipes out our old nature and gives us a new life of relationship with God. It's not a formula, but it is the only way. Jesus said in the Gospel of John 14:6, "I am the way, the truth, and the life. No one can come to the Father except through Me" (New Living Translation). And that can happen for you, right here, right now. Just pray from your heart:

Lord Jesus, I come before You right now. I acknowledge the deep areas in my life that I need help with. I know I'm a sinner who has not lived right up until now.

As good as I've wanted to be, I have failed too often to count. Today, I ask you to forgive me. I accept by faith that You died on my behalf. This day I ask You to be the Lord of my life. Make me the holy, complete person You have always desired me to become. I surrender my life to You now and I thank You for the new life that is even now mine in You.

Congratulations. Get to know the Lord by spending time with Him daily as you would a new friend. Get a bible, one that you can easily understand, and get to know the Lord more intimately. Finally, link up with other believers. Find a good fellowship that worships Him with abandon, values His word as perfect truth, and feels more like family than you've ever known. Don't be discouraged when you see other believers making mistakes. Remember this isn't about being perfect, it's about becoming perfect! There is a big difference.

And finally, happy fishing in the deep places with the presence of the one who is overjoyed to be with you and brings you freedom.